Acknowledgments

This book would not have been possible without the fantastic support I've had from some key people:

To Gill, my wife, who has supported and encouraged me – even when things got tough. You are my best friend and the love of my life.

Louise and Livvey the beautiful girls in my life – this is for you.

Penny James, who always believed in me.

My friends and colleagues who road tested the book and gave me frank feedback – Shirlene Adam, Joy Wishlade, Brendan Cleere, Jeremy Thornberry, Pete Weaver, Alison North, John Lewis, Ruth James, Helen Phillips, Jane Chipp, Simon Lewis, Greg Dyke, Adrian Priest.

Keith Ellis who gave me his expertise.

All those authors and trainers who I've had the pleasure to read or meet and have contributed in no small way to this work.

My deepest thanks to you all.

ABOUT KEVIN TOLLER

Kevin was born and bred in Somerset where he still lives and works.

He is married to Gill with a daughter, Louise, who is studying at Edinburgh University.

Kevin has worked in the public sector for many years and is currently a Strategic Director – part of the top management team – for his local council.

His first book – "The Time of Your Life" came from a long interest in time management and a frustration at not being able to find the book he really wanted on the subject. He decided to write that book and seeing that others found it helpful, decided to get it published.

He uses his time management techniques to fit many interests into his life. In addition to his very full time job he plays classical and electric guitar, teaching both to a range of students. Playing in a classical guitar ensemble has given an opportunity to raise funds for local charities.

Kevin also loves to paint - mostly watercolours, but is dabbling in oils and acrylics. He began painting when he found that his first love of photography wasn't giving him the images he wanted. The advent of digital photography has changed all of that and his love of photographing landscapes has returned. The photograph on the cover of his book is one of Kevin's.

To keep fit Kevin runs raising money for various charities each year. He recently completing his first half marathon – rather further than his more usual 10k distance.

He says time management helps him do all of this and stay (reasonably) sane!

ISBN: 978-1-84944-064-6

British Library Cataloguing in Publication Data.
A catalogue record for this book is available from the British Library.

Published by UKUnpublished

UKUnpublished
.co.uk

www.ukunpublished.co.uk
info@ukunpublished.co.uk

THE TIME OF YOUR LIFE

By

Kevin Toller

INTRODUCTION

I have been a connoisseur of time management techniques for many years. My bookshelves are crammed with books on the subject and I've been on countless courses and seminars. But I've always been frustrated. I've gained something of value from each and every book, magazine article or event. Most gave me more ideas, tools, tips or techniques than I could handle at the time, and as a result many of them remained untried. Most of the books were read, and then went back on the shelf. Most of the courses and seminars were great, but then I went back to work the day after and the real world kicked in.

Does any of this sound familiar?

Over the years more and more parts of what I'd learnt did begin to gel and come together into something that seemed to work. I began to share it with others, and it seemed to work for them too.

I was still frustrated though. I couldn't find the book or the course that set out clearly the essentials of time management in a way that I could use and which I knew would make a difference. I wanted something that would not only help me day to day but also longer term in achieving my goals – whatever they were.

Then, one day whilst meditating, it came to me. If it's not out there, then write the book yourself. And just perhaps, it may be the book that others are looking for too.

Well, finding the time to write the book within an already busy work schedule (I wasn't about to give up the day job) and with all my other commitments wasn't easy. But using the skills from the book, it proved to be possible – after all, here's the book!

So, if you want to sort out your time management – and are prepared to work hard to do so – then, this is the book for you.

I hope you enjoy using it – and more importantly enjoy the vast benefits of improving your time management.

Kevin Toller
March 2010

CONTENTS

WHAT THIS BOOK IS ABOUT

Let's be clear to begin with – you can't manage time. It's just not possible. It's like being in the sea and believing you are in control of the water – it's all around you but you can't manage it. All you can do is decide which strokes to use and then do something. Your actions determine whether you sink or swim.

It's the same with time – can you get more of it? Can you bank some and save it for a rainy day? If you've wasted some, can you get it back? No matter what you do you will never add 1 more minute to the day. You get the same 24 hours as everyone else, no more, no less.

All you can do is decide what you are going to do and then do it.

If only it were quite that easy. If it was, you wouldn't have bought this book – you would be perfectly happy that you were getting done everything you wanted to; you wouldn't perhaps be snowed under at work or at home; or feeling overwhelmed with too much to do and too little time to do it in. Putting this right is not rocket science. Deep down, most of us – and I suspect you too – know exactly what we need to do to put all this right. Unfortunately, all too often, we just don't do it.

However, you already have the key part of the solution – you. In fact, there is no other person who can sort this out for you. Your success in managing your way through life is 100% entirely down to you, and no one else. My aim in writing this book is to enable you to recognise the tools you can use and give you the chance to put them into practice to make a real difference for you.

You won't find lots of time management theory; there are plenty of excellent books available that can give you all you'll ever need in that area. You also won't find millions of ideas, tips and tricks that leave you thinking "where on earth do I start". You also won't read this book like other books and put it on a shelf to gather dust – it's not designed to work that way. This book will be your constant companion for the next few months. If you are prepared and committed to work with it, then you are guaranteed results – it's as simple as that.

If you're still reading, I will assume you've made a real commitment to get things sorted. Good. This book is designed to be worked through step by step. You can read all the way through if you want, to get the overall picture, but the best way is to start at the beginning and work your way through to the end.

I understand, however, that perhaps you've picked this book up because you feel that you are already sinking rather than swimming. If this is you, turn to the "Quick Fix" section. It's not a long term solution, but it will help you get back on an even keel as quickly as possible. You can then start to look at the habits you'll need to develop to maintain this for the long term.

Unlike other books, this one will sit on your desk, or in your briefcase, or on your kitchen table until you finish it – and that will be some months. Managing yourself better doesn't happen overnight.

Like all of us you will need to create new habits – because the steps in here need to become second nature to you – and to create a new habit you need to behave in the new way every day for several weeks. You're going to create lots of new habits, but you're not going to overload yourself by trying to do it all at once – so be prepared; your life – and you - will now begin to change beyond recognition. Things will never be the same again.

Good luck and enjoy the ride!

THE BASICS

You already fill 24 hours of every day with something, whether it is work, leisure, exercise, family commitments, sleep or collapsing in front of the TV.

Imagine that there will never be any more work coming in your direction – no more emails, phone calls, letters, memos, demands from the boss, or meetings….

Now, think for a moment about all the things you have to do and want to do. Very roughly estimate how long it will take to do all those things – even without anything else coming in to take up your valuable time. For most of us, it will be weeks or even months.

So, you already have more than enough to keep you occupied for weeks, and realistically the world isn't going to stop and wait while you get on with it.

The harsh reality is that you are always going to have far more to do than you will ever be able to do. You already have no "spare" time – even if your diary has blank spaces in it, you know it's really already full with all the things that need doing.

Just think too, that staying behind to work that extra hour tonight isn't really going to make much of a dent in the weeks of work that will always be there for you.

This means that to do anything new or different you will have to change something else first, and you don't have many choices.

You can choose:

- Not to do something – basically stop doing it
- To do it more efficiently, so that it takes up less of your time
- To do it less well (a real challenge to perfectionists!)
- To get someone else to do it for you (delegation really)

That's it. There really aren't any other options for you. I said it wasn't rocket science.

Time management then is simply about taking control over what you do next.

To be effective your new way of working needs to become second nature – so you don't even need to consciously think about it. If you've been driving for a while, you don't ever really think about all those complex actions you take – you just do it. Thinking about driving actually makes it difficult, doesn't it? Your time management needs to get to the same level of habit.

A new habit is going to take you about a month to establish, and ideally you will only work on one at a time. You will work on the new behaviour everyday. You won't allow any exceptions to the new habit, because any exception will undermine all the good work you will have already done.

STEP 1 – WHY?

To make any successful changes we have to understand what it is we are trying to change and why. Let's start by looking at why and find out what is going to motivate us to do something differently.

We've seen that no one but you can improve your time management.

Therefore, it is important to understand why you want to do this – what's in it for you?

Think very carefully about why you want to do this. When you succeed and free up, let's say 2 hours every day, what are you going to use that time to do?

Here are some possibilities to get you thinking:

Why do I want to manage my time better?	
• To reduce my stress levels • To feel more in control • To achieve more • To feel less rushed • To relax	• To feel healthier • To stop feeling overwhelmed • To minimise wasted time • To be able to do things properly • To feel calmer

What do I want to do with all the extra time I gain?	
• Learn to play an instrument • Spend more quality time with my family • Take up a sport • To work for promotion • Go on holiday • Achieve a specific ambition or dream • Learn new skills • Earn more money	• Start exercising • Run a Marathon • Begin a new hobby • Take on more responsibility • To study • Do voluntary work • Take on another job • Spend time with friends

This serves a number of critical purposes:

• You will clarify exactly why you are making this effort;

• You will have real, personal targets to work towards;

• You can refer back to this when the going gets tough, to remind yourself why it is all worth doing;

• You will be less likely to get sidetracked into frittering away all your hard earned gains in doing more of the same.

Write your reasons down on the next pages.

It's also worth writing them down and putting them somewhere really visible so that you can see them and be reminded of them frequently – put them on your office wall; on the bathroom mirror; turn them into your computers' screensaver. Seal them in an envelope and give them to a friend – ask them to post the envelope back to you in six months time.

The possibilities are endless, limited only by your imagination.

Why do I want to manage my time better?

What do I want to do with all the extra time I gain?

STEP 2 – WHAT?

Human behaviour is naturally habitual. If we do something often enough it becomes a habit and essentially we really don't need to give it conscious thought. Habits will almost be unnoticeable. This is great if the habit works in your favour, but not so good if it doesn't.

You will already have a number of time management habits – some of which you will need to bring out into the daylight so that you can see them and perhaps change them. Do you recognise any of the following habits that won't be helping you?

- Frequently working late
- Procrastination
- Welcoming interruptions
- Interrupting others
- Indecisiveness
- Focusing on the things you can deal with quickly
- Trying to do everything yourself
- Too many meetings
- One crisis follows another
- Always late for meetings

[handwritten notes:]
- Doing things in too much detail
- "Priority inversion"
- Over-planning + under-doing
- Unclear time boundaries
- Vague prioritizations

Your aim will be to ensure that the habits you use are helpful – either by replacing those that currently work against you, and/or by introducing new ones.

What are your current habits – which ones do you want to keep and which do you want to change or replace?

What are my current time management habits?

STEP 3 - MAKING CHOICES

Now that you have identified some really good reasons why you want to make better use of your time, let us turn our attention to making choices.

We simply cannot do everything, so we do have to make choices. Every time we make a choice we are saying "yes" to something and "no" to something else. Not always simple or straightforward.

How can we make it easier?

Remember when we started to look at how your time is spent we noticed that you already have all of your time occupied with something, and you have much more to do than you could ever complete today? Recognise, therefore, that every time you take on something new – a new activity, hobby, piece of work, responsibility and so on, something else has to give or go. This means that you will have to drop something else, or not commit as much of your time and attention to it as you did previously.

Is the new thing that important to you? That's a choice you have to make. That in itself can be difficult unless you are clear on what your values and aims are.

Your values are those things that you hold dear, they are fundamentally and vitally important to you. Your values will change over time. You can establish what they are right now.

What are my values?

To determine your current values, write a list of everything that is really important to you – it might include:

- attributes like integrity or honesty
- people issues - having friends, relationships or family
- material issues – having a home or money
- developmental issues – your own personal or professional growth
- spiritual issues – your beliefs
- action issues – travel, sport, exercise

This list is not meant to be exhaustive, it's just to give you a few starters. You may find you have quite a long list at first.

Everything that is important to me right now

Integrity

Reliability

Being deeply in touch with myself
& acting out of that

Honouring my inner voices —
enough to hear/acknowledge them —
then to take them into a/c when
acting.

Getting fit — exercise

Yoga
Meditation
Chi Gung
Music — learn bongoes + flute
Walking
Gardening

When you have your list take each item in turn and ask yourself why is it important to you. This will drill a little deeper into what your value really is. When you have that answer, ask again why that is important to you – drilling still deeper. Keep asking yourself the question until you can go no further. This will then be one of your values. You will almost certainly find that many of the items on your original list will drill down to the same basic values.

When you have distilled your basic values write them out again.

Why? + How? Questions

My Values

Read them over and live with them for a while. Do they feel right for you? Some will be more important to you than others, can you decide which are the more important – these will be the values that drive you and your behaviours day to day. You may be able to identify perhaps 4, 5 or 6 values that are the crucial ones for you.

What are my aims?

Your aims are all those things you need and want to do. Some will be short term, others long term. To determine your aims, think about your life in the distant future – say 10 or even 20 years' time.

- What will it look like?
- What will you be doing?
- Where will you live?
- Who will be around you?
- What will you have achieved?
- What will you be working on?
- What dreams or ambitions will you have?

Describe this in as much detail as possible.

My life in _____ year's time

So what have my values and aims got to do with time management?

Your values and aims drive you and help you decide what to spend your time on. Whenever you get a request to do something new, extra, or whenever you feel you want to do something different, ask yourself whether it fits with your values and aims.

If it does, then go ahead. If it doesn't, then stop and think about why you might want to do this. Is there a compelling reason to do this activity that doesn't fit in with your values, or takes you no nearer to achieving any of your aims?

Stop at this point.

Complete the descriptions of your values and aims.

Put a reminder in your diary for 6 and 12 months time to review it.

When you have done this, move on.

STEP 4 – WHAT DO I HAVE TO DO?

Having decided why you want to improve your time management, you now need to look at the scale of the task.

To begin with, make a list of everything you are required to do or want to do. Don't worry at this stage about any sort of organisation to the list; just get everything you can think of on to it.

If in doubt, it goes on the list.

It is vital that you include absolutely everything. This list is going to form the basis of the very heart of your personal time management system and the more complete it is, the easier the next stage becomes.

You may well be surprised at how long the list is. Don't panic though, in the next steps you will start to bring it under control. For now, just knowing the size of the beast is a huge step forward. Remember that time management is about choices – a long list simply means you'll have a lot of choices to make.

Now obviously it is going to take a bit of time to prepare this list, and you may well be saying "but I don't have the time, which was the whole point of getting this book".

This is, however, one of the single most important steps towards you achieving your goals. Just for a moment go back and look at the reasons you wrote down for why you wanted to do this. Are they not reason enough to invest a little time now to gain those rewards?

You will know that if something really critical to you came up, you would find a way to make time to do it. This is one of those times.

Also, there is really not much point in reading any further until you have done this list. So, if you can't do it right now, decide exactly when you will do it, book the time in your diary, commit to it and then leave the book open at this page on your desk, or table or in your briefcase until you've done it.

When you've made your list, move on quickly to the next step, before it changes.

**Make a list of
everything
you have to do or want to do.
Include
everything
you can think of,
no matter how big or small.**

STEP 5 – MAKING IT WORK FOR YOU

You now have a list of everything you need to do or want to do. Whilst being able to put boundaries around the demands on your time is important, in itself it's not going to help you manage your time any better. To do that you need to turn the list into something useful. We'll simply call it your Action Plan.

There is a template on the next page. Put each one of the items on your list into the appropriate box on the template.

This Action Plan will form the core of your time management system. In one place you will have a complete record of everything you need to do. To be effective you will need to keep it up to date – your mind will continue to worry about forgetting things until it realises that you have it all under control through your action plan.

Don't give your mind the chance to undermine your good work by leaving things off the plan.

You will see a number of significant changes happening in the coming days as you start to use this action plan:

- You'll stop worrying about forgetting to do things;
- You'll stop forgetting to do things;
- You'll begin to make choices about what to spend your time doing;
- You'll find sorting out your priorities becomes easier;
- You'll get distracted less often;
- You'll start to delegate more, and better;
- You'll start to achieve more of what you want;
- You'll begin to get a reputation for doing things;

- Your stress levels are likely to reduce;
- You'll feel much less overwhelmed;
- You'll get satisfaction when you can start seeing things being completed;
- You'll never feel stuck for something useful to do;
- You'll begin to feel more in control of what you are doing.

There are some refinements you can build into the Action Plan very quickly that will improve its effectiveness for you. These are listed immediately after the template.

As you get familiar with the template you may find ways of making it work better for you. Do feel free to customise it.

This, then, becomes the first new habit for you to learn. Use the Action Plan every single day for the next month. Keep it up to date. This is crucial – as soon as it becomes incomplete it loses any value to you.

New Habit Number 1

Use the Action Plan every day

ACTION PLAN – Today's Date

DO NOW Things that have to be done NOW	**PLAN TO DO** Things that need to be done, but don't need to be done today. This is the to do list for the future and will probably be the largest section of your action plan. Aim to book time in advance in your diary to do these things.
DO TODAY Things you want to do today or have to be done today – put in priority order. This is really today's "To Do" list. Note they often won't all get done!	**DON'T FORGET TO DO** These are the things that are longer term, need to be done but aren't priorities.
TELEPHONE Calls you need to make	**READ** Those key documents you must read

AWAITING ACTION BY OTHERS

MONITOR	**NO IMMEDIATE ACTION**
These are things that other people (staff, colleagues, whoever) are doing – either things that have been delegated to them or you are waiting for them to do something before you can proceed further. The date when the matter left you for them is noted too, to make future chasing easier. This section ensures that anything you're involved in which you need to keep an eye on is not overlooked.	Things which you are involved in, usually with others, but where you are not required to do anything at present.

It's easy to reproduce it in your favourite word processing package.

Kevin Toller

ACTION PLAN – Date.....................

DO NOW	PLAN TO DO
DO TODAY	DON'T FORGET TO DO
TELEPHONE	READ

AWAITING ACTION BY OTHERS

MONITOR	NO IMMEDIATE ACTION

Refining Your Action Plan

Ask yourself the following questions of each item before you add it to the plan:

- Does it need to be done? Be ruthless. Delete anything on the list that you do not intend to do at some point. If you are not going to do it, it doesn't need to be there.

- Does it need to be done by you? Delegate extensively. You should do only those things that only you can do.

- When does it need to be done?

    o **Right now** – if it's going to take less than 5 minutes AND you are going to do it right now AND you know you will finish within that time, don't put it on the plan, just do it. Everything else goes on the plan.

    o **Later** – decide what needs to be done next to progress the item, decide when you are going to do that, schedule the time and put it in the appropriate section of your Action Plan. One thing is for certain, if you don't decide when and commit to the time in your diary, then it is very unlikely to get done.

- For all of the items in the "Plan To Do" section, decide what needs to be done next to progress the item, decide when you are going to do that, and schedule the time.

- Obviously, your Action Plan is going to get extremely unwieldy if you are involved in multiple major projects. Bear in mind that you can't "do a project"; you can only do actions, which eventually make up a competed project. In such circumstances make sure you have detailed action plans for each project – which you would normally keep with the project papers – and simply transfer the next actions to your main Action Plan in the appropriate sections. This ensures that you only have one master copy to think about.

Stop at this point.

Keep using your Action Plan every day for the next month.

When you are happy that it has become part of your normal way of doing things, move on.

STEP 6 – WHAT DO I DO NEXT?

By now you will have a good understanding of the scale of your workload. You have organised yourself so that you know which tasks need doing at different times and are beginning to get organised to achieve the things you want to.

To really start making a difference on enhancing your achievements – actually doing things and getting them off your Action Plan completely – we need to take a look at what you are going to do next. This is about handling priorities.

Your Action Plan, as we have seen, probably contains several weeks' worth of work for you to do. Clearly, therefore, you can't do it all today, or even tomorrow. This means that you have to make some choices. Your achievements and reputation will depend to a very large extent on the quality of the choices you make.

You can find plenty of systems that strive to give some apparent objectivity to establishing your priorities, often asking you to score each task against a range of factors – perhaps including importance, urgency and impact. The problem with this is that often you will find several of your tasks have the same priority, so you are no further forward in deciding what to do next. This is a good time for procrastination to set in – and we'll look at that in more detail later.

In any case, remember that if you still have too much to do, making decisions on your priorities is really only deciding what it is you are not going to get done.

The reality is that in most key areas you can only work on and give your full attention to one item at a time. Deep down, you know at any time what that specific item is. Trust your instincts.

Knowing what you should do and doing it, though, are very different. You'll have already seen that managing your time better is largely about self-discipline. Working on your priority areas is exactly the same.

If you think about it for a moment, once you have decided what is the most important thing for you to do right now, then everything else must be secondary and of less value or importance.

Logically, therefore, why would you do anything else? Later, we will look at why you will often find yourself doing anything but the task you know you should be doing.

For now, however, you can start work on developing your second new habit – getting things done.

New Habit 2 – Getting Things Done

Think of the impact on you, your workload and your reputation if every day you were able to achieve the one key, most important thing that you chose to do.   That's what we'll focus on next.

Decide what is the most important or valuable task for you to do tomorrow. Go with your instincts.

Get everything possible ready the night before, so get any papers, tools and workspace ready. If you work at a desk get everything off your desk unless it relates directly to the task you have chosen.

When you arrive for work, start your chosen task immediately.

This is where it gets hard. Immediately means right now.

> It doesn't mean after checking your in tray.
> It doesn't mean after checking for new emails.
> It doesn't mean after standing chatting for 10 minutes at the coffee machine.
> It doesn't mean after anything else.

It means right now.

Why? Simply because once you get caught up in anything else it is highly unlikely that you will get to spend as much time as you'd hoped on the thing you chose to do.

You may not even get to it at all.

There is an old Irish proverb that says:

If you have to swallow a frog, try not to think about it. If you have to swallow two frogs, don't swallow the smaller one first.

Or, if you prefer –

Swallow a toad in the morning if you want to encounter nothing more disgusting the rest of the day. (Nicolas Chamfort – French writer)

New Habit Number 2

Decide on the most important thing to do tomorrow, and then do it first.

But What Do I Do Now?

This approach deals very nicely with getting the most important tasks done, and it's easy to say that when you have done the most important task you simply move on to the next most important task and so on.

The real world doesn't quite work that way though does it?

In reality, you will get interruptions, distractions and crises. You will find yourself with unexpected windows of opportunity when a meeting gets cancelled, your train or plane is late, you arrive early, or someone is late for their appointment with you.

As an effective time manager, you need to develop flexibility, especially to make use of those windows of opportunity.

To help decide what to do next consider the following:

What could you do where you are now?

The answer is likely to be different depending on whether you are at your desk or at the airport, for example. There's no point trying to do something that you just don't have the right tools or facilities to handle effectively – no matter how important it is.

How big is the window?

Do you have 2 minutes whilst you've been put on hold, half an hour before your next meeting, or all afternoon?

How do you feel?

Are you energised and raring to go, or are you flagging and running on empty?

Choose

Having considered the above, what is the most important and most effective task you could do next? Do it.

Stop at this point.

Keep doing the next most important thing every day for the next month.

When you are happy that it has become part of your normal way of doing things, move on.

STEP 7 – WHY IS IT ALL SO DIFFICULT?

You have now developed the first two important new habits – Action Planning and Doing the Most Important Things.

By now you will have realised that whilst the tools you have to improve your time management are easy to understand, they are far from easy to use effectively. Procrastination is usually one of the main culprits.

Procrastination occurs every time we put off doing something we know we should be doing now. We can even procrastinate sub consciously. There's always a payback though, when we hit that moment when there is no escape and it just has to be done, and usually there's no longer enough time to do it properly. Even worse is when we realise that it's now too late to do it at all.

So why do we procrastinate?

There are only a few fundamental reasons, but all can be a very deep part of each of us:

- I cannot do it
- I might do it wrong and be a failure
- I might do it right and be a success
- I'll be able to do it better later
- It's too daunting to start
- I just don't want to do it

So how can you address these?

Inevitably, you only overcome procrastination by doing something. The steps you have taken will already be helping you to beat procrastination, but you can refine these even further:

Firstly, decide precisely what it is you want to achieve.

Now you have an important decision to make – you have to make an agreement with yourself. Much of our bad feeling about procrastination comes from the fact that we really don't like breaking agreements with ourselves. Yet that is exactly what procrastination does to us. We make an agreement with ourselves to do something and then don't do it. We can then beat ourselves up for not doing so.

To overcome procrastination you only have three choices to make:

- you can choose to make an agreement with yourself to do it – and then get on with it;

- you can choose not to make an agreement. – choose not to do it and don't make a promise to yourself that you can't or won't be able to keep.

- You can choose to renegotiate with yourself – agree to do it in a different way or at a different time.

The choice is yours.

If you choose to do it:

- Write it down. The writing helps to ensure that you are really clear about what it is you are going to achieve.

- Set yourself a deadline. Without a deadline, it won't happen.

- Work out what needs to be done.

- Break it down into small steps so that each is achievable.

- Create a plan.

- Do the first thing on the plan that needs doing.

- Then do the next action.

- Do something towards your objective everyday until you succeed.

> **Remember you can only run a mile one step at a time, but you can't finish unless you stay the course.**

STEP 8 – WHERE DOES ALL THE TIME GO?

By now, you have a good understanding of what you need to do with your time to effectively and efficiently achieve your objectives. You are getting yourself better organised so your capacity to do things is increasing.

You will also be aware that, despite your best efforts, you are not yet making the best use of the time you have. So where does it all go?

Can you remember precisely what you did yesterday or the day before? Can you identify where your time was wasted or used inefficiently? Are you confident that you spent the right amount of time on the right things?

If you answer is "no" - then completing a Time Log is the answer.

If your answer is "yes", then completing a Time Log is the answer (because I guarantee you'll be surprised and learn something to improve your time management).

Time Logs get a bad press – they take too much time; it's hassle; or you forget to do them.

But, if you don't know where your time is being spent – and you almost certainly don't – then how are you going to begin to control it?

You will almost certainly be surprised at how little of your working day is spent on the really productive and high value work that you want to do.

Time Logs don't have to be time consuming or complex. There is an easy way. You also don't need to do them everyday forever, a few days or even a week when you feel the need will be fine.

New Habit Number 3

Complete a Time Log.

New Habit 3 – Completing A Time Log

Write down what your goals are for today. You can lift these directly from your action plan if you like.

Against each, write down, as precisely as possible, the time when you expect to complete each item today.

Record each activity you do during the day. That means every activity including the coffee breaks, socialising, bathroom visits, daydreaming, working out what to do next, celebrating success, as well as real work!

The easiest way to do this is make a note each time your activity changes. Do this as you go along during the day – don't save it for every 15 minutes, or do it at the end of the day. The only way you'll get a useful record is by doing it as you go along.

For each activity, record what it was, how long it took, who was involved and anything else you might feel is relevant.

A search on the Internet will give you quite a number of electronic and web based tools to help, if you prefer to operate in this way.

A paper-based example is also included on the next page that you can recreate in your favourite word processing package.

Time Log	
Date	
Today's Goals	**Deadlines**

Activity	Start	Finish	Time Spent	Who else was involved	Planned Y/N	Notes

Analysis

At the end of the day, analyse your day's activities. You can do this at the end of the week as well.

Your analysis might include all or some of the following, though the list is not meant to be exclusive. Use whatever parts are useful to you, and add anything else that you find of particular value. Your main task is to be rigorous in your analysis – going easy on yourself will do you no favours at this point.

- What progress did you make against your goals?

    o Did you start and finish each task when you expected to – if not, what was the reason and does it still seem like a good reason at the end of the day?

    o Did you get to spend enough time on each of your goals? If not, what were the reasons? What got in the way or prevented you from doing so? Looking back, were they good reasons? Could you have done anything differently that might have helped?

- How much effective time did you spend at work?

    o How much of your time was spent on valuable, productive activities i.e. the things you are being paid to do?

    o How does this compare with the number of hours you spent at work?

- o Divide the time spent doing valuable work by the time you spent at work. This will give you a useful figure as a guide to how efficiently you are working. Whilst there's no right answer and 100% is probably unattainable, does your figure suggest anything to you? If, say, it is below 80%, could you make some changes to become more efficient?

- How did you manage interruptions?

  - o How many were there?

  - o What were the main types of interruption?

  - o Who caused them – was it you or someone else?

  - o Can you see any patterns – do interruptions occur at specific times, when certain activities are happening, or involve certain individuals?

- Where did procrastination strike?

  - o Can you identify what caused it?

  - o Were you able to overcome it?

  - o How could you overcome it in future?

- What did you achieve during the day?

  - o Were your achievements linked to your goals?

  - o Did you celebrate your successes?

- o Did you get caught up in low level/low value work?

- o What distracted you, and why?

- Were they any occasions when your time management got out of control?

  - o Why did it happen, could you have prevented it?

- How was your time spent between the different areas of your life – was there a balance that you feel happy with?

  - o If there was an imbalance, why was that? What could you have done differently?

- Are there any changes you can make?

  - o Are there activities you can reduce or eliminate?

  - o Are there any activities you can delegate?

- What lessons can you learn and apply in future?

  - o Write those lessons down and commit to learning them.

Time Log – Lessons Learned

Stop at this point.

Complete and analyse a Time Log for the next week.

Put a reminder in your diary for 3 months' time to do it again.

When you have done this, move on.

STEP 9 – LEARNING TO JUGGLE

Your diary or schedule is the key tool for helping you control what you do with the time you have.

Whatever you do will use up some of your time. Therefore, if you want to do anything you will have to give it some of your time.

You can, of course, trust to chance. That you will somehow find the time, it will miraculously appear. But by now, you already know that you have much more to do than you will ever have time to complete. You have choices to make – often tough ones – about how you are going to spend your time. Unless you specifically allocate time to those things you want to achieve, there is a good chance they simply won't happen.

Your diary is the key to this.

In addition, if you don't schedule your time and plan your days, others will plan them for you and happily take up your time.

It doesn't really matter whether it's paper based or electronic. The important thing is that it exists and that you use it to your advantage.

Using a diary is about scheduling time in advance to do the things that:

- You have to do.

- You want to do.

- Are unexpected.

The last item is included on purpose. It is very easy to schedule your diary so tightly that the moment anything unexpected happens everything falls apart. Let's be realistic here. The unexpected does happen – frequently. So, the diary can help you prepare for that and give you the capacity to respond when you need to and potentially without all of your best laid plans falling down in ruins.

Your diary, used flexibly, gives you the tool to juggle your commitments to fit the prevailing circumstances.

New Habit Number 4

Use your diary to your advantage

New Habit 4 – Use your diary to your advantage

What should go into the diary?

Meetings

• All the meetings you need to attend.

• Include any travel time.

• Any preparation time for meetings – let's say you have a regular Monday morning management meeting and that there are always papers to read beforehand that you get on Thursday. Book all of the meetings in your diary AND book yourself enough time on Friday to read the papers. Or if you have appraisals to do, schedule not only the time for the actual appraisal, but also the time needed for you to prepare and write up the results.

- After some meetings there will be specific work you know in advance you'll have to do – writing up the appraisal reports for example. Book in time to do that too.

- Book regular meetings (and the attendant preparation/ travel slots etc) as far in advance as you can.

- Beware of what I call the "conveyer belt days" – those days where the day starts with a meeting, which leads directly into the next one, and the next one, and the next and so on. It's like stepping onto a conveyer belt first thing in the morning and hoping you are still vertical when you step off in the evening. These days will happen – even with the best laid plans – but should not be your norm. So when you diarise meetings, do your best to ensure adequate spacing between them and break them up with other activities where possible.

- Rather than planning on being on time, identify when you need to stop working on something in order to ensure that you are on time for the next appointment.

Regular Tasks

- Almost inevitably you will have regular tasks to do that come round at certain times of the day, week, month, quarter or year. They are inevitable, and they all take up your time. Schedule the appropriate time in your diary well in advance. Then you'll know that you have the necessary time already set aside to do them when they arrive.

- You can even do this with the dreaded email – firstly turn off the beep that tells you a new email has arrived, and then plan to look at your emails at specific times to suit you. Take control of when you deal with your emails rather than letting them control you.

- Similarly, you can schedule appropriate times to make your phone calls.

- Block as many routine jobs together as possible, and then deal with them in batches. Your aim is to spend the minimum time doing that essential but low value work.

- Set aside amounts of time to do the small things that you still have to do, but don't let them become the major things that you spend your time working on. Remember the 80:20 rule – the Pareto Principle - which means that in anything a few (20 percent) are vital and many (80 percent) are trivial. These small things are part of the 80% that only deliver 20% of your results.

- Get yourself off any subscriptions or email distribution lists that don't add value to you. If you don't have time to read them now, perhaps they really aren't that important.

- Keep your maintenance tasks up to date – when you finish with a file, for example, put it back in the right place ready for next time. Similarly, put any tools back where they belong and ready for action – if your stapler runs out, get new staples, don't wait until you need it next time.

- Have a clear out. Plan ahead, say once a quarter, to have a good clear out of stuff you don't need or use. Purge files so they only contain what you need.

Real Work

- You remember all those things on your "Plan To Do" list? Each needs time allocated to it in your diary. Book in the appropriate amount of time.

Contingencies

- Book this in as "Contingency Time" or "Keep Free" or a meeting with yourself. You are not planning specific work at these times, they are your windows of opportunity. You will use them to juggle your commitments when you have to; to enable you to catch up where things have overrun or not been done; to give space for managing the unexpected.

- Don't skimp on allocating this time – aim for a minimum of 2 half days every week – and book them well in advance. When you first do this, you may have to wait several weeks for the first one to actually appear, but it is worth the wait. This is one of those areas where electronic diaries are so useful – you can so easily book yourself a "keep free" for every Tuesday afternoon from here until eternity! You also know, that if the worst comes to the worst and you don't have anything unexpected to fill the time, you've still got plenty on your "Plan To Do" list and you know exactly what needs doing next, so it's easy to make valuable use of the time.

- Make it a rule that no one overwrites these times without your express agreement AND without putting an equal alternative time in your diary.

You

- Build in time to look after yourself, exercise, recreation, health check ups and so on.

- If we don't develop as individuals we don't progress. Schedule yourself time for your own personal development, however you like to do that.

- Lunch and refreshment breaks – despite the fact that these are so easy to simply work through, they are essential in helping reduce stress levels.

Holidays

- Book time for you to take significant breaks away from work.

- If you like to take the odd day off, book them in well in advance – you can always choose not to take them when they arrive, but you know how hard it is to take a day off at short notice.

- Book yourself some clear space for immediately after you return from your holidays – it always takes a few hours to get back on your feet, so give yourself that time. You'll be back on top, in control and firing on all cylinders much faster as a result.

Quiet

- Some people like to build in perhaps an hour each day of quiet uninterrupted time where they can just get on with the really important things that they want to do. You may like to play ambient music in the background. This can help keep things calm, and can also be a very good signal to others that you really don't want to be interrupted right now. You'll be amazed at what you can achieve by doing this.

Thinking

- In the rush to get things done we so often overlook the value of reflecting on our achievements and thinking about the future. Build some thinking time into your diary to do just that. You'll know what is appropriate for you – is it 15 minutes a day, an hour a week, half a day a month, a full day every three months?

Finally, be wary of putting high energy items back to back in your diary. It doesn't matter if they are mentally, physically or emotionally demanding – too many of them one after the other will lead to exhaustion and poor performance. A little bit of planned space will make all the difference.

Stop at this point.

Schedule your diary, and learn to keep it organised so that it helps you.

When have done this, move on.

STEP 10 – PLANNING

By now you will have gathered that planning is rather fundamental both to the effective management of your time and - probably even more importantly - to achieving the things you want to achieve.

Planning – particularly in the context of projects - can be extremely complex. Here, though, we are concerned with keeping things as clear and straightforward as possible. For our purposes in improving your time management, planning consists of only three stages:

- Decide what to do

- Decide when to do it

- Do it.

This latter stage is the key. A plan is no more than a paper exercise unless you put it into action. Conversely, action without a plan is no more than random activity.

When planning, it is easiest to work from the big picture down to the smaller details. This means we start with what we want to achieve then gradually break that picture down into meaningful and achievable activities – things you can actually do.

Having the bigger picture also makes it much easier to see whether the things you are doing or are being asked to do really add any value to achieving your goals. Where they don't add value, it becomes much easier for you to make choices – and to say "no" when appropriate.

Writing your goals down is fundamental to your success. That may seem strange at first, but writing them down helps to ensure that you are really clear about what you want. It helps focus your attention. You will also find yourself being more committed to achieving the goals, and with commitment comes action. Once you start taking action on your goals you make progress, and progress will eventually lead to completion and success.

If you have some of your goals written down, and others not, you will very quickly see that the ones you make progress on are those that are written down.

New Habit Number 5

Plan

New Habit 5 – Plan

Start with your goals. What do you want to achieve? Don't worry about timescales at this stage – it doesn't matter whether the things you come up with are days, weeks, months or years away. The aim is to be clear on what you want to do. Use the opportunity to look at your whole life – the following categories, whilst by no means exclusive may help you think this through.

I Want To Achieve	
Job/career	
Family and personal relationships	
Health and well being	
Leisure	
Spiritual	
Financial	
Travel	
Education and personal development	

Creativity	
Community or voluntary service	

Filtering

You may have found that there is a lot you want to do.

Go back over your list. Think about the first item. What would it be like to have achieved this? Create a vivid picture in your mind where you can see what it is like, what the impact is. Does it feel good? Do you feel motivated to work to make it happen? If so, move on and do the same for the rest of the things you want to achieve.

If suddenly it doesn't feel so good, or it really doesn't motivate you, ask yourself if you really want to achieve this. Perhaps you can remove it from the list, or if not ask yourself what it is going to take for you to feel good about this.

By now you may have filtered a few items out and your list may be a little shorter.

When?

Next, review each item on your list and decide when you would like to have achieved it by. Be as specific as possible.

How?

If you are going to turn any of these goals into reality, you will need to work out how to get there. Don't worry if at this stage you don't know; having committed to it, your brain will work on it anyway. In many cases, though, you will be able to identify a whole range of steps you can take which will lead to you either achieving the goal, or will take you at least some way along the right road.

For each goal, write down the steps you identify and create an Action Plan, with deadlines wherever possible.

Doing It

Each month choose which of the actions you are going to do towards achieving your goals. Using your new habits, write them down and schedule when you will take those actions.

Review

It is useful to review your goals and their associated actions at least annually. This gives you the opportunity to:

- recognise the progress you've made
- review and learn from any areas where progress wasn't made
- make necessary adjustments
- consider whether any goals have become obsolete
- consider whether you have any new goals

I want to………………..	By………..

Action Plan	
Action	**When**

Stop at this point.

Complete your list of goals and actions.

**Put a reminder in your diary for 12 months' time
to review it.**

**Put a reminder in your diary for the beginning (or end if
you prefer)
of each month for the next year
to review the next actions you intend to take.**

When you have done this, move on.

STEP 11 - DEALING WITH THE UNEXPECTED

Life doesn't happen according to plan – the one thing that is guaranteed is that the unexpected will happen, and usually when you least expect it!

With your new found capabilities in planning and scheduling, you are no doubt finding yourself to be much better organised. But does the unexpected throw you off course? Are there too many crises, or perhaps your job largely consists of one crisis after another? Is dealing with the unexpected causing you difficulties in achieving what you really want to? Are you still getting frustrated because you are spending so much time dealing with fighting fires and not getting to your real goals?

Here is another way in which your Time Log can help.

Look back over your Time Log. Focus specifically on the unexpected happenings and crises.

Before you look at handling them, consider what actions could have been taken that would have meant you didn't have to deal with them in the first place – prevention is always better then cure:

- Was it foreseeable, and therefore could you have done something that would have meant that it never happened?

- If it was unavoidable, was there anything you could have done which could have enabled you to deal with it at a more appropriate time?

- Did it have to be dealt with?

- Could you have reduced the impact in any way?

- Could you have delegated responsibility for dealing with it?

Once you have established the real core of the unexpected tasks, how much of your time was spent dealing with them - 10%, 25%, 80%? Does that feel typical for you?

Let's say that after careful consideration you conclude that typically, you spend 75% of your time dealing with the unexpected or unavoidable crises (you shouldn't have to deal with avoidable crises of course!).

If you are sure that this is all unavoidable, and that it all adds value to what you are doing, then we come to a harsh reality. 75% of your time, on average, is going to be spent on such issues.

That means only 25% of your time will ever be available for everything else you want or need to do. Now is the time to revisit your diary. Does your diary reflect that reality or not? You are probably going to have to revisit your plans and be more realistic about what you can achieve with only that amount of time available to you.

One thing is certain, and that is if you fill your diary with appointments and other work, knowing that you are going to spend 75% of your time fighting fires it doesn't take an Einstein to work out what happens next…

Now, by its very nature the unexpected doesn't turn up on time, to a pre-planned schedule. You can't, therefore, book 2 hours time in your diary for next Monday afternoon to deal with an unanticipated crisis that hasn't yet happened and almost certainly won't now happen on Monday afternoon. What you do know is that at some point you will spend time dealing with these things.

If you know you are going to spend 75% of your time, for example, dealing with the unexpected then 75% of your diary needs to be blocked out to give you the space and capacity to deal with it when it does arise. In this example, that probably means booking several hours every day, when you will not be available to do anything else.

You then use your juggling skills to move your availability around to meet the demands put on you. The key is that now you have the windows to be able to juggle your time. You will find that, mostly, you will now be able to respond to the unexpected and still deliver everything else you aim to do.

There will be those days when it all goes to pot, but you will have further windows in your schedule that will enable you to get back on top and in control really quickly.

If you are lucky enough to find that today there were no crises, then enjoy the opportunity to use those windows of time to make real progress on the next important item on your plan – make a real difference today!

Step 12 - Managing Interruptions

You have already identified that dealing with the unexpected means allowing time for you to do so.

Some interruptions are inevitable – the boss will drop by and give you some more work (don't they always!); one of your staff will want some guidance; a colleague will drop by to ask you a question and so on. Ensuring that your schedule has flexibility will help you to deal with those interruptions that must be acted upon.

Get into the habit of completing your work on time – other people will hassle you far less and so you'll get less interruptions from them.

As you will by now have gathered though, when interrupted, the first question will always be – do I need to?

Can I have a minute?

The drop in visitor is often one of the main culprits for interruptions. How often have you heard "could you spare me a minute?" – and you know that it's never going to be just a minute, probably half an hour if you are lucky.

So, how can you best deal with these interruptions effectively?

The first, and probably the most important step is to learn not to say "Yes" immediately. Often our natural reaction when somebody says "can you spare a minute" is to say "yes". Think about this for a moment. By saying "yes" you have instantly decided that their request is of a higher priority than whatever it was you were already doing – and you don't even know what they want yet…..

Only when you know what it is they want can you deal with it effectively and appropriately.

The first question to ask is "what is it about?"

Once you have the answer you can then decide whether to:

- Deal with it there and then

- Defer it to another time – ask them to come back later when it is more convenient

- Suggest someone else who could deal with it for them – i.e. delegate it

- Encourage them to find their own answer – i.e. give some guidance

Of course, many of us create our own interruptions too. Your time log completed earlier will help you to see how and why you do this, which in turn will help you find solutions to reduce this tendency. It will also show you if you are a major source of interruptions to others……

STEP 13 – SAYING NO

You will have gathered that managing interruptions, like many aspects of time management, is about making choices.

We simply cannot do everything, so we do have to make choices. "The "yeses" are often fairly easy, but most of us have problems with saying "no". It is so final, it emphasises that we have made a choice, a decision, and it might hurt, offend or upset someone.

Every time we make a choice we are saying "yes" to something and "no" to something else.

If you decide not to proceed, than you are saying "no". The most effective way to say "no" is by doing so simply and clearly. You are not obliged to justify yourself, though by all means give a reason if you wish – but never an excuse. Be clear, you may find yourself being vague and saying "I might" or "I'll see what I can do" when you really mean "no". To the other person, "I might" and "I'll see what I can do" mean "yes". Now it becomes even harder to say "no" when you fail to turn up or deliver.

If you mean "yes", say "yes" and recognise that this means you will be saying "no" to something else you had planned or wanted to do.

STEP 14 – MEETINGS AND YET MORE MEETINGS

If meetings have a place anywhere in your life then you already know how much of a time waster they can be. Your time logs will show you in detail how much time you spend in meetings – and your diary will show you how you manage yourself in relation to them. Both, however, will often underestimate the impact of meetings on your precious time, as we tend to ignore:

- Preparation time – all the papers you need to read, or write before a meeting;
- Any travel time to get to the meeting – even if the 10.00 meeting is a few minutes walk from where you are, do you leave at 10.00 (or indeed at 5 past, because no-one else gets there on time)?
- Recovery – the time it takes to re-energise your self after a meeting before you are truly ready to tackle whatever comes next.
- The work you acquire at the meeting.

Meetings Analysis

Just for the next week keep a record of all the meetings you attend in whatever role:

Meeting	
Why did we meet	
Did it achieve our aims	
Was there an agenda	
Did we keep to the agenda	
How long was the meeting	
Did it start on time	
Did it end on time	
Who was there	
How much did your time cost	
How much did the meeting cost	
Would you be willing to pay for that meeting for those outcomes	

We can often attend a meeting that appears to be productive only to find that when we meet the next time, nothing much has actually happened.

Usually this will be because:

- someone did not realise that they were meant to take some particular action,
- "other things got in the way" – which really means "I wasn't really committed to do this and didn't give it any priority".

This simply adds to the ineffectiveness of meetings, yet is possible to overcome by ensuring real clarity over:

- what action is required,
- when is it required
- who is required to do it.

Do not, under any circumstances, let a meeting finish without ensuring that everyone present is completely clear on each of these three points and is committed to delivering any actions required of them. Any vagueness will almost certainly result in no action being taken.

Some Tips for Successful Meetings

Use an alternative

From the perspective of managing your time, often the most effective meetings are the ones you don't go to! Ask yourself, is there any other way of achieving the needed outcomes that would be quicker and more effective? Perhaps an email, telephone call, tele or video conference would be appropriate. If so, use it.

Decline

If you really don't have to be at a meeting, then decline – don't go. Think of all the more important things you could be completing.

Leave

How often do we sit in meetings when the item we need to be there for is over, or won't be reached for some time yet? Make an agreement with the chairperson that you will leave after your item, and/or will not arrive until the time when your item is likely to begin. Then use your time to achieve something important. Obviously, if you are the chairperson then perhaps you need to be there throughout – but don't assume this. Could someone else chair part of the meeting for you? Perhaps it might be more appropriate for them; or perhaps it might be part of their development.

Punctuality

If you are the chairperson, make it a habit to always start your meetings on time, and don't waste time recapping when the late arrivals appear.

Recapping simply wastes the time of everyone who has taken the trouble to be there on time, and panders to those who weren't.

Once this becomes a habit, others will naturally recognise that they will be missing important parts of your meetings if they arrive late.

If you are a meeting participant, then make it your habit to arrive on time too.

Punctuality with finishing times is also key. As the chairperson, be clear about when the meeting will finish. One of your tasks as chairperson is to manage the meeting so that it finishes within the allotted time. Nobody will mind if you finish early, everyone will mind if you finish late.

Be Prepared

If you are chairing a meeting, make sure that when you arrive you are prepared – don't waste everyone's time by being unprepared and disorganised. Ask yourself, would I respect and feel confidence in someone who clearly doesn't know what they are doing here? Your reputation and credibility is at stake.

If you are a meeting participant, you will make the most effective contributions, and thus make the most effective use of your time at the meeting, if you are also well prepared.

Focus

On the assumption that the meeting is taking place because it has a purpose, ensure that this is then the focus of the meeting. Keep discussions firmly to the point.

Action

If the meeting is effective there will almost certainly be some actions required. This is where it is crucial to be precise and clear – what is going to be done, by when and who is going to do it? As I've mentioned earlier, do not allow the meeting to finish until everyone there is totally clear on the actions.

Take these tips, together with any lessons you have learned from your analysis of meetings you have attended, and identify the new habits that will help you become more effective at meetings. The template following might help.

Meetings – My New Habits	
The New Habits I need to learn and apply	**How the New Habits will help make meetings more effective for me**

Stop at this point.

Analyse the meetings you are involved in for the next week.

Identify the new habits you need to learn

and apply to make meetings more effective.

Apply those habits for the next month.

Then carry out another review of meetings for a further week.

You will be able to see clearly the improvements you've made

and may notice new lessons too.

Only move on when you have completed this review.

STEP 15 – DELEGATION

Many of us find delegation really hard to do well, yet it should be one of the cornerstones to our success. Management in its fundamental sense is simply about getting things done through others. This means that unless you delegate, you are not really managing.

But we often resist delegation, and there can be many reasons for this. Here are some examples:

- it's easier to do it myself
- it takes too long to delegate
- they won't do it the way I would
- I'll only have to redo it
- they are already busy and won't like me piling more work on
- I like doing whatever the task is

In the context of making the most valuable and effective use of your time, delegation simply means if someone else can do it, then they should and you shouldn't. Your efforts and energy need to be focussed on those things which only you can do. This is where you really add value and make a difference.

New Habit Number 6

Do nothing that you can delegate

New Habit 6 - Delegate

Think about yourself. What prevents you from delegating more?

My reasons for not delegating more

Let's now look at some of those reasons and analyse them for what they are. You can do the same for any other reasons you have added.

Reasons for not delegating	Think About
It's easier to do it myself	Is this the most effective use of your time? Consider delegation as a long term investment. If you do it yourself, you will also have to do it yourself the next time, and the time after that, and the time after that……..Train someone else and you'll never have to do it again.
It takes too long to delegate	Once again, if you train someone else to do it well, your investment now will pay you back huge dividends.
They won't do it the way I would	This is almost certainly true. They will do it their way. It might even be better than your way. Be clear on what outcome you want from the delegation, but let them do it their way. Let go a bit.
I'll only have to redo it	On occasion this just might happen, but if you delegate well, it will be a rarity.
They are already busy and won't like me piling more work on	Or they might not be. You can always help them to reprioritise and manage their time better.

I like doing whatever the task is	This is often the hardest one of all. We just don't like to let go of things we enjoy doing, even if it is now really more appropriate for someone else to be doing them. Learn to let go, move on and find new things to enjoy which are of greater value to you.

You will now understand what is holding you back from delegating more. Let us now look at the positive side of delegation – what do you need to do to delegate well?

Strangely, there are very few "rules" to effective delegation.

- Delegate everything you possibly can – aim to make yourself obsolete so that you can move on to more important things - if someone else can do it, let them

- Be clear yourself on what outcome you want from the delegation and communicate that precisely – so make sure that the other person knows exactly what outcome you want. This may include what you want, the standards you expect, monitoring arrangements and any constraints – deadlines, budgets, resources and so on.

- Ensure that the person knows whether you are asking them or telling them. Asking gives them the option to say "no thank you", telling is a command.

- Ensure that they have not only your authority to do the job – including using their initiative and making decisions - but that they also have the necessary skills, knowledge and abilities.

- Follow up progress. What you delegate is only as important as the importance you put on it. If it's not worth you following up……is it worth someone else putting time and effort into doing it? The chances are if you don't show interest in how it is going, it won't actually happen.

- If a deadline is missed, focus on when it will be done by – not why it was missed. Don't accept excuses, but keep moving forward.

- Don't accept poor quality work – this merely sets the standard for next time. Delegation is about developing others and their capabilities so they can add more value too. Use these opportunities.

- Praise and reward for a job well done.

The Quick Fix - Getting Out of Overwhelm

You may well have the best of intentions to sort out your time management, but perhaps right now you are deep in overwhelm, with far too much to do and not enough time to do it. You feel snowed under and can't find the way out.

This situation only arises because right now you are over committed – you have agreed to do too many things. I know that sounds harsh, but there is no more to it than that.

This is when a quick fix is called for. In reality, a quick fix won't help you for very long, but if you really are in trouble right now this is the quickest and most effective solution:

- Decide what timescale your current overwhelm covers – is it just today, this week or this month. Any longer than this and a quick fix isn't going to help you – you will need to go straight on to "The Basics" section.

- Write down the things you want and need to achieve during this timescale.

- Write down all the actions you need to take to achieve those things.

- Estimate how long it will take you to complete all of the actions you have identified.

- Add 20% to your estimate (we all underestimate how long things will take us).

- Add up how many hours you need to complete everything.

- Calculate how many hours you have available in your timescale.

- Divide the hours needed by the hours you have.

- Assuming this is more than 100%, you can now see clearly just how overcommitted you are.

Now you have some choices to make. It should be clear to you that you simply cannot do everything that you have identified. Trying to continue to do all of them almost certainly means doing none of them well at all.

Alternatively, you may just not get to some of them – and you can guarantee that if others are expecting you to deliver and you don't, that's far worse than renegotiating a new deadline with them

As you are in an overwhelm situation, the choices probably won't be easy. Look back at your list of things you need and want to do in this timeframe. Decide for each one:

- Does it need to be done right now?

- Can all or any of it be delegated to someone else?

- Is there a quicker, alternative way of doing it?

- Can you leave it until later and if so, does anyone else have to know or agree to this?

- Can you delete it completely, and if so who do you need to say "no" to?

Having made these decisions you should be much closer to being able to complete those things that are left on your list. If you are not yet close enough, go over the process once more, being even more rigorous.

Use this approach anytime you get into overwhelm, but remember it's only sticking plaster and won't solve the underlying issues that you will need to address to more consistently and effectively manage your time. For that, return to the "Basics" section

SUMMARY OF YOUR NEW HABITS

New Habit Number 1 -   Use the Action Plan every day

New Habit Number 2 -   Decide on the most important thing to do tomorrow, then do it first

New Habit Number 3 -   Regularly complete and assess a Time Log

New Habit Number 4 -   Use your diary to your advantage

New Habit Number 5 -   Plan

New Habit Number 6 -   Do nothing that you can delegate

A FINAL WORD

I suggested right at the outset that you can't manage time. Remember the swimming in the sea analogy, where all you can do is decide which strokes to use and then use them?

Well, hopefully, you now have several strokes to choose from, and they are all working. You have some sound new habits which will help keep you afloat and moving in the direction you want to go. Now is not the time to become complacent however. In the sea, once you stop swimming you don't remain afloat for very long.

So, do review your progress regularly, and keep those habits working for you.

I wish you well.

Kevin

SUGGESTED FURTHER READING

Do It Tomorrow, Mark Forster
(Hodder & Stoughton, 2006)

Do Less, Achieve More, Chin-Ning Chu
(ReganBooks, 1998)

Eat That Frog! Brian Tracy
(Mobius, 2004)

First Things First, Stephen R. Covey, A. Roger Merrill with Rebecca R. Merrill
(Simon & Schuster, 1994)

Get Everything Done And Still Have Time To Play, Mark Forster
(Hodder & Stoughton 2000)

Getting Things Done, David Allen
(Piatkus Books Ltd, 2001)

How To Get organised When You Don't Have The Time, Stephanie Culp
(Writer's Digest Books, 1986)

More Time, Less Stress, Judi James
(judy Piatkus Publishers Ltd, 2002)

The Mind Gym – Give Me Time, Octavius Black and Sebastian Bailey
(Time Warner Books, 2006)

The Now Habit! Neil Fiore
(Jeremy P Tarcher; Rev Ed edition, 2007)

The Personal Efficiency Program, Kerry Gleeson
(John Wiley & Sons, 2004)

The Time Trap, Alec Mackenzie
(AMACOM, 1997)

Time Management for Unmanageable People, Ann McGee-Cooper with
Duane Trammell
(Bantam Books, 1994)

Time Management From The Inside Out, Julie Morgenstern
(Hodder & Stoughton, 2000)

Index

Notes

Notes

Notes

Notes

Notes

UKBookland gives you the opportunity to purchase all of the books published by UKUnpublished.

Do you want to find out a bit more about your favourite UKUnpublished Author?

Find other books they have written?

PLUS – UKBookland offers all the books at Excellent Discounts to the Recommended Retail Price!

You can find UKBookland at www.ukbookland.co.uk

Find out more about **Kevin Toller** and his books.

.CO.UK

Are you an Author?

Do you want to see your book in print?

Please look at the UKUnpublished website:
www.ukunpublished.co.uk

Let the World Share Your Imagination

Lightning Source UK Ltd.
Milton Keynes UK
27 July 2010

157489UK00002B/26/P